Planning to Protect Your Money and Your Family

Table of Contents

Introduction

Family legacy and financial planning is not everyone's favorite topic. In fact, I'd be willing to bet most of us spend more time trying to avoid it than just doing it.

As frustrating as it can be to think about the planning we need to do to protect our money and our families, it is a necessary evil. The best way to reach your goals in life is to put plans to paper and put those plans into action.

The best way to ensure you and your family meet your life goals is by planning for your financial future. The best way to ensure your children, spouse, or other family members are protected if you can't take care of them, is to put plans into place now. Don't leave your planning up to the Courts. Take control and make the decisions that are right for you!

I created this book to help you understand the steps and necessity of financial and family legacy planning so you can get started as soon as possible and secure you and your family's future!

GETTING STARTED

Janet was a 35-year-old single woman who lived paycheck-to-paycheck. There never seemed to be enough money once the bills were paid and the groceries ordered. She knew she needed to set some money aside for savings and for retirement, because she would love to retire one day, but she just didn't know how.

Janet constantly felt the pressure and stress of not having enough money. She would watch her bank account total dwindle down to zero every month. She felt like each day she got up, went to work, came home, and never had anything to show for her long hours.

Janet did not have a budget. She didn't think much from day-to-day about what she bought or if she needed to buy it. She just checked her online account occasionally to make sure she could go out to dinner with her friends or order that pizza for supper on Friday.

Janet finally decided she was tired of going around and around in circles. She wanted to stop having to worry about money. She wanted to pay off her debt. She wanted to make a plan so she could retire one day. But, Janet didn't know where to start.

If Janet's story sounds familiar to you, this guide can help you get on the right track. So, where do we start?

The best place to start is always at the beginning. With financial planning, simply getting started is the first, and hardest, step.

Financial planning can be boiled down into 8 basic steps. Each one is as important as the others. When starting your plan, it is helpful to set aside a little time every day to work on the steps of your plan.

A little time can go a long way. You will likely find that setting side just ten minutes a day can help you finish one step within a week or two. So, make a plan to plan!

BUDGET, BUDGET, BUDGET

Janet had so much to do each day. She came home and crashed on the couch, tired from a long day at work. Often, she would curl up with a glass of white wine, and her dog, Buster. She would order take-out from a restaurant down the street and binge watch her favorite streaming app. She didn't want to think about anything when she got home.

But, making a financial plan doesn't have to be hard or time-consuming. If you take just a few minutes a day for a few weeks, you can get yourself on track to save for an emergency and retirement.

We've all heard it at least a hundred times before. The key to financial success is keeping track of what comes in, what goes out, and ensuring your expenses are less than your monthly income. So, let's talk about how to do that!

Step One: Determine Income and Expenses

The best way to track your finances is to review your last 3 or 4 months of bank statements. Sit down, with a pen and paper, and write down the average of the last 3 months expenses for every expense. For example, rent/mortgage, utilities, food, entertainment, etc. Everything should be captured.

If you do not have a bank account, you'll have to do this the old-fashioned way. You can carry a notebook with you and track every purchase you make. Do this for 3 or 4 months. Then, average your expenses to get an idea of your monthly expenses for each item.

Next, look at your monthly income. If you're self-employed, or a contractor, your income may vary. You need to take that into consideration when making your budget. Are there times of the year you make more than others? Budget off of your lowest income to be sure that you don't overextend yourself.

Once you know your income and expenses, analyze whether you're spending more than you have coming in. If you are, it's time to make some changes. What those changes are is up to you. Should you get a second job to cover expenses? Are there some items you're buying on a regular basis that are luxury items you can live without? Decide the best route to balance your budget for you and your family and put that plan into action.

Step Two: Set Goals

Here's the fun part! Think about what you want in the next 20 to 30 years of your life. Don't think broadly, such as I want to travel. Be more specific.

You want to paint a vivid picture of what your future looks like. Do you want to pay for your children's college education? Do you want to drive a Maserati? Do you want to backpack through Europe?

Do you want to own a home? If so, how big do you want that home to be? When do you want that mortgage paid off? How much do you want to save for retirement?

Dream your dreams and set them down to paper. If you don't have them on paper, you can't make your plans to reach those goals.

Step Three: Insure Your Future

It can be hard to understand why insurance is a necessary expense, until the day you need it and don't have it. If you don't have a family, on top of your home, health, and auto coverage, you'll want to consider disability insurance.

Disability insurance allows you to receive a portion of your income if you're ever disabled. Disability insurance helps you stay afloat during disability.

If you have a spouse, and/or children, you'll also want to think about life insurance. Life insurance will help your family pay the bills if you die and they lose your income. A great insurance agent can help you figure out the exact amount of insurance you will need.

Generally, the younger you are, the cheaper insurance is. So, start planning your insurance policies sooner, not later! Insurance is a great way to keep your financial plan on track when something unexpected happens.

Step Four: Know Your Credit

Credit is a necessary evil in today's world. Even if you don't use credit cards, and it's highly advisable to avoid them as much as possible, you will need credit to take out loans for cars, mortgages on homes, and often, even to qualify for rental properties.

You can get free credit reports online each year. You can access them directly through the major three credit companies, TransUnion, Experian, and Equifax. You can also pull them through a free online service, annualcreditreport.com.

Step Five: Make a Savings Plan

Your first major goal is to set aside about $1,000 for emergencies. Emergency water leaks or car repairs can derail your financial goals if you don't have emergency funds available to cover them.

Once you have an emergency fund, free up some of your income for savings. Your ultimate goal is to have 3 to 6 months of your total expenses saved up so that you can weather any storm. A job loss or other major crisis is likely to resolve within 3 to 6 months, so you will rest securely knowing that your expenses are covered during those already stressful crises.

Step Six: Invest

After you have an emergency fund saved up, you can focus more on investing. There are many investment options available to you. You can look into mutual funds, bonds, stocks, or real estate, to name a few.

Think about your goals and how investing aligns with those goals. If you are interested in stocks and mutual funds, consider speaking to an advisor who can help you manage the funds, or teach yourself about the stock market if you're more hands-on.

If you have a retirement savings with your employer, start working to put as much away as you can by law, and through your budget, each year. The benefit of employer-sponsored plans, is they usually have a matching system, which allows you to get more bang for your buck. Take advantage of your company's benefits.

Step Seven: Review and Revise

Your plan is fluid. It moves and changes with your life and circumstances. Don't make a plan, leave it, and forget it.

Revisit your plan from time to time, especially after big life changes. Marriage, divorce, birth, and death can all affect your goals and future. Your plan is made to grow and change with you, your family, and your lifestyle.

Consider planning meetings with your trusted advisors each year to review and revise your plans with their help. Their involvement can also help keep you accountable for putting your plans into action.

Step Eight: Anticipate Your Largest Goals

Be sure to allow yourself more than one way to achieve your dreams. If you want that boat in 15 years, you will want to consider investments that grow quickly and will allow you to pull out the money for your boat at that time, in case you haven't saved enough.

If you're looking to retire, you need to know what age you plan to retire, how much you'll need to live off of, and how much you need to save to reach that goal. Talk with a trusted advisor to get your strategies safely in place.

Family Legacy and Estate Planning

Larry was married for 15 years. He and his wife, Blanche, chose not to have children. He ran a successful roofing business and was an avid fitness fanatic.

One day, Larry's wife got a call that Larry had a heart attack while running on the treadmill at the gym. He died instantly.

Blanche was reeling with grief while she tried to navigate funeral and medical expenses. She worried about how she would maintain the mortgage on her home and the loan on her vehicle without Larry's income.

They owned some bank accounts together, but Blanche and Larry married later in life. Blanche gave up her own home and moved in with Larry into his $250,000 home when they got married.

Blanche and Larry didn't think much about it. They thought since they were married, the home would be Blanche's if something happened to him.

A few months after Larry's death, when Blanche was finally starting to get her head back above water, Blanche decided she needed to move. The memories of Larry and the size of the home were just more than she could handle. She wanted a smaller home for herself and hoped to put the extra money from the house's sale back for retirement.

Blanche spoke with a realtor who realized the home was only in Larry's name. Now, in order to sell the property, Blanche had to go through probate and spend thousands of dollars and precious time to transfer the property to her name.

Larry's parents had died some time ago, and Larry only had one sibling. Larry didn't talk much about his brother and hadn't seen him in years. But, Blanche learned that Larry's brother would not only have to receive notice of the probate, but under Oklahoma law, because Larry and Blanche did not have any estate planning documents, Larry's brother would be entitled to a portion of the equity in the home.

Blanche's plans of using the money she earned from the sale for retirement were shattered. Because she couldn't find Larry's brother, she had to pay her attorney even more money to sell the home through the probate. Larry's brother's portion was turned over to unclaimed property for the State.

Whether you are single, married, a parent, or a Stepparent, you need a family legacy or estate plan to ensure that your assets go to who you want them to go to. If you don't, the Court will make that decision for you. Most of us don't want that.

PLANNING TOOLS

Last Will and Testaments

Last Will and Testaments, also known as Wills, allow a person to designate who gets what on the death of the creator. Wills must follow certain rules and formats to be valid. Often, Wills made on legal document sites do not follow the rules for a valid Will.

Though Wills allow the maker to decide who gets what, a Will still has to go through the Court process of probate to transfer the assets to the recipients. The probate process is time consuming, expensive, and, depending on the family dynamics, it can be messy.

Every family member that could inherit from the deceased if the deceased didn't have a Will has to receive notice of the proceedings. Though rare, this can lead families to fight over the assets and drag out the Court process even longer than usual.

Recipients do not receive their inheritance until the Court process is completed. And when it is, recipients will receive their inheritances outright without restriction.

Trusts

Trusts are contracts between the creator and the "Trustees" the creator chooses to manage the Trust for him or her if the creator is incapacitated or dies.

A trust does not go through the Court process of probate. So, the assets are kept private and the distributions are handled in a private setting. Uncle Joe won't have to find out what your spouse or kids inherit and would have a difficult time contesting the Trust.

Trusts also allow you to place restrictions on distributions. So, if you have a young child, instead of the child receiving all assets at 18, you can restrict the assets not be given to the child until the child is 25, or whatever you choose.

One thing families with Trusts misunderstand is that a Trust is only as good as what you put in it. If you, your document production service, or attorney forget to place a bank account or property into the Trust, that property will have to go through the Court process of probate to transfer title.

Durable Powers of Attorney

Durable Powers of Attorney allow individuals to choose someone who can act on their behalf if they cannot make decisions for themselves. These documents are contracts as well. So, the individual can choose whether the person they choose to act, or "attorney-in-fact," can act immediately (such as in cases where people may be out of the country for an extended time) or only in the case a physician deems the maker unable to make decisions for his or herself, or "incapacitated."

The maker can allow the attorney-in-fact to act for them in medical decisions and/or financial decisions.

They can make those powers to act as broad or as limited as they would like.

Durable Powers of Attorney are best when someone is leaving the country and needs someone to act for them for a period of time and to prevent a family from having to go through the Court process of Guardianship if the maker can no longer make decisions for him or herself.

Guardianship is a Court process where a loved one for someone who cannot make decisions for and/or care for his or herself asks the Court to allow the loved one to make decisions for the incapacitated person. The Court will determine if the person is, in fact, incapacitated and will decide if the loved one is qualified to care for the incapacitated person.

The Guardian has to ask permission to sell or buy assets for the incapacitated person and file Annual Accounts with the Court. The process is expensive, time-consuming, and often stressful, as people generally do not like to go to Court and have to miss work or other obligations to be able to make the Court hearings.

Advance Directives

Advance Directives for Healthcare are the only documents in the State of Oklahoma that allow another person to withhold life-sustaining treatment for the maker if the maker is unable to make decisions for his or herself. The Advance Directive has 3 parts: (1) The Living Will, (2) Healthcare Proxy Nomination, and (3) Transplantation decisions.

The Living Will takes you through specific situations where you would be faced with the decision of whether to withhold life-sustaining treatment. You make choices for what you would want in each situation.

The next section allows you to name a Healthcare Proxy. This is the person who would make decisions about whether to continue life-sustaining treatment when you couldn't make the decision for yourself in situations other than those covered in the Living Will.

The Transplantation section allows you to choose if you want your organs to be donated for transplant surgery for others or for research purposes.

Parents With Young Children

Mark and Abby are in their mid-twenties. They married about 3 years ago. Until now, they have been travelling and going out with friends almost every night. But, recently, that changed.

Abby found out she's pregnant- with twins! Now, they are worried about how they will afford their wonderful bundles of joy. There's so much to buy!

They need 2 cribs, 2 swings, 2 car seats, and diapers galore. Though they both make a good living, they find themselves questioning if they can afford to live in their apartment, or if they'll need to move to another part of town. And, now their lifestyle will change too.

As long as Abby and Mark plan, they'll be ok. When your plans include young children, there's a lot to consider. As all parents know, children add a lot of expenses to your budget.

In 2017, the Department of Agriculture completed a study that found raising a child born in 2015 to adulthood costs middle-income families $233,610 per child! The calculations include housing, food, transportation, and clothing. They do not include private or college education expenses. With inflation, it is likely those costs have increased since the study was done.

BUDGET FOR BABY (OR BABIES)

If you don't already use a budget, and you have a child on the way, be sure to go back to the beginning of this Guide to help you set up a personal budget. Once you have done that, you will need to factor in extra costs that come with having a baby.

And, those costs depend on a lot of factors. First, will you use cloth diapers that you can wash? Or, will you use disposable diapers? Second, will your baby drink formula or not? Third, what about clothes? Do you have close friends and family members who are able to pass on some hand-me-downs? If not, how much will clothing cost?

A good place to start is to look at your own budget and see where you can make some changes and reduce some expenses. Then, you will need to decide what you can afford to do for baby. You can't buy Gucci and Prada baby clothes on a Wal-Mart budget. So, be honest with yourself and your significant other about what you can afford.

Child Care

As a new mom, I was shocked by the costs of child care for infants and young children. Be prepared to pay $1,000 - $2,000 per month on daycare expenses for a newborn. If you plan to have a two-income household, put this additional expense into your budget now.

Another issue to consider with children is whether you want to pay for additional educational expenses. Do you want to put your children into private school throughout their education? If so, you need to estimate what those expenses will be and start planning when your baby is still preschool aged.

How about college? Do you intend to pay for your child's college education? If so, you will want to start saving now. Some options to explore include ROTH IRAs set up for child's educational expenses, or a tax-advantaged 529 plan.

ROTH IRAs will not receive tax benefits, but the money can be saved for your child to use for any purpose. A 529 plan will not be taxed, but the money can only be accessed, tax-free, for qualified educational expenses for your child. Talk to professionals to figure out which plan is best for you.

PLANNING FOR YOUR CHILD IF SOMETHING HAPPENS TO YOU

Do you have a plan in place for your children if something happens to you today? Would your babysitter or nanny know what to do if you didn't make it home?

For many of us, the answer is no. If you do not have a plan in place, you'll likely face the same problems as Mary's and Trey's families. Guardians

Mary was on her way home from work when she got into an accident. Though she survived, she was unconscious and taken to the hospital from the scene. Her husband, Mike, was out of the country on a business trip. Mary did not make it to the daycare to pick her two young boys, Alex and Bo, up.

The daycare workers tried to call Mike, but they couldn't reach him. When Mary didn't show up an hour after the daycare closed, the daycare called the police. The police had no choice but to take Alex and Bo into custody.

Alex and Bo were not only worried about their mother and what had happened to her, but now, they were forced to stay overnight with strangers. Alex and Bo cried all night and kept asking questions about Mommy and Daddy.

Mary's neighbor, Alison, watched the boys frequently and had two boys of her own that Alex and Bo played with often. Alison wanted to take the boys and care for them in Mary's absence, but because Mary and Mike did not have a plan in place, Alison had no legal authority to care for the boys.

Mary finally gained consciousness the next morning. She was able to get the hospital to contact the police and track down the boys. They brought them to the hospital, where they met Mary and Alison the next afternoon. But, the boys were still scared and traumatized from the 18 hours they spent in the State's custody.

If you want your children to be taken care of if you are not able to care for them, you have to have the proper plan in place.

<u>The Fix</u>

The first, and most common, step to helping you make a plan for your children if you can't care for them is to name a Guardian in your Will. This Guardian must be someone you trust to care for and raise your children as you would.

What many families overlook, however, is the gray area in between. Naming a Guardian in your Will, though helpful, does not remedy the situation Mary's family experienced. If you merely have a Guardian named in a Will, the police will still have to take your children into custody if you cannot be found until the Guardian named in the Will can learn what happened to you, find the Will, and arrive in your town to pick your children up. Not the best solution.

We recommend naming a temporary Guardian nearby who can care for your children immediately if your long-term Guardian is unavailable. We also recommend sharing your plans with your childcare providers so that they call your temporary Guardians before they call the police if they cannot find you.

That way, your children are in a safe, comfortable place with people they know. Though the comfort and safety won't end their fears and trauma, at least it will minimize it as much as possible.

Asset Distribution

Another consideration when planning for your children when you can't take care of them yourself, is planning for the possibly considerable assets that may be left to them before they are adults.

A good example of what can happen if you don't have a plan for distributions to your children is the story of Trey.

Trey's parents died in a car accident when Trey was 10. Trey's parents were on their way to a vacation out of town when a semi crossed the center line and hit them head on. Trey's parents had a plan in place, so Trey did not have to spend time in CPS care, but they did not make a plan for distributing their life insurance policies. They named Trey outright as a contingent beneficiary if something happened to them.

Trey's grandmother, Dorothy, cared for him while he was growing up. Because Dorothy was the Guardian for Trey, she received the life insurance policies on his behalf.

Though Dorothy was a wonderful caretaker, she wasn't very good with money. She immediately bought a larger home for her and Trey. She also bought herself a new car. She told herself these purchases benefitted Trey because she would be able to better care for him with these purchases. She didn't put any money back for him.

Dorothy also had a significant gambling problem when she was younger. For a long time prior to Trey's parents' deaths, Dorothy hadn't gambled. But, the temptation of the money she received for Trey was too much to handle. She sank back into her old habits. She wound up blowing the rest of Trey's inheritance at the casinos.

Trey did not have anything left when he turned 18 and applied to college. Because he couldn't afford college, he chose to go to a trade school. Though he was able to pull himself up from his bootstraps and make a great life in his trade, that is not what his parents wanted to happen to his inheritance.

Trey's parents would have liked Trey to be able to use his inheritance to purchase a home, pay for college, get married, or invest for his future. They did not want his money to go to the local casino.

The Fix

When parents place their assets into a trust, or name their trust as a beneficiary of certain assets, they have the chance to say where those assets go and when. Trey's parents knew Dorothy was not good with money. They didn't want everything to go outright to her on Trey's behalf, but they did not realize Trey could not receive money if they died before he was 18.

Trey's parents could have placed their assets into a trust and named a Co-Trustee who could invest on Trey's behalf while making sure Dorothy could handle the added expense of raising Trey. The Co-Trustee would have to approve the purchases of the new home and car and distributions taken from the trust.

If you have concerns about someone else managing your child's money if you die while they are under the age of 18, or if you have concerns about your children receiving one large lump sum if you die when they are young adults, a trust is the solution for you.

BLENDED FAMILIES

If you have children from a previous relationship and are in a new relationship, you have unique considerations for your family legacy planning.

Tanya and Ben had a wonderful relationship. They met just after Ben divorced the mother of his children, Rita. Tanya didn't have children of her own, but she loved Ben's children, Jenny and Emma, like they were her own. Jenny and Emma even called Tanya mom.

Ben's marriage to Rita fell apart because Rita developed a drug addiction. The addiction changed Rita and changed the way she interacted with her daughters. Because of her issues, Ben had full custody of their children and Rita was given custody every other weekend. Rita rarely came to pick the girls up.

One day, Ben was climbing the oil rig at work. He lost his footing and fell. Tanya received the call that Ben wouldn't make it home. Tanya immediately looked at Jenny and Emma and wondered what would happen to them.

When the police arrived at Ben and Tanya's home later that day, they realized that Tanya was not the birth mother of Jenny and Emma and had no legal authority to care for them. They were able to reach Rita, and despite the fact Emma and Jenny hadn't seen her in almost a year, the police took Jenny and Emma to their mother's home.

Tanya was devastated. She raised the girls with Ben. Rita had been inconsistent and unreliable. The girls wanted to stay with Tanya, but it didn't matter. Legally, Tanya had no claim to them.

Tanya filed for Guardianship in Court and spent the next year fighting for custody of the girls. She eventually found enough evidence of Tanya's addiction to win and bring the girls home, but in the meantime, she spent countless sleepless nights and thousands of dollars trying to protect them.

If you're in a blended family, be aware that the Stepparent has no legal authority to care for the children in the biological parent's absence. Also, unless there are extreme circumstances, the other biological parent will gain custody of the children and control of the children's inheritance if the deceased biological parent doesn't properly plan.

The Fix

A trust and nomination of Guardian are the best documents to protect blended families. Though the police would have still reached out to Rita in this situation, in the meantime, or in her absence entirely, the girls would have stayed with Tanya. Though a Court battle for custody may still have been a problem, the chances Rita would return to seek custody if she hadn't already had the girls in her custody are much smaller. Tanya's chances of not having to battle Rita increased.

Moreover, if you are concerned about another parent's ability to manage assets, or fear they may not allow a continuing relationship with a Stepparent, you could name the Stepparent as the Trustee of the children's trust. At a minimum, such a designation would require the other parent to be in contact with the Stepparent to access the children's inheritance. Naturally, the Stepparent would be able to continue contact with the children.

Conclusion

So many Americans are living paycheck to paycheck. They're caught in an endless cycle where one emergency could cause them financial ruin. Putting a plan in place will help you end that cycle and live the life you want.

Families are so caught up in their day-to-day lives that they don't think about the bigger picture. What could happen to their children and their assets if they didn't make it home tomorrow?

The only things certain in life are death and taxes. Though thinking about what will happen when we die can be difficult, we all need to have that conversation.

Call us today to set up a consultation to learn what will happen to your assets and family under your current plan.
###

About the Author

Attorney Sarah C. Stewart focuses her estate planning practice on helping families understand and plan for their specific goals throughout their lifetimes. Whether your family is blended, single-parent, life-partner, or traditional, Sarah's knowledge and expertise allows her to help you navigate the confusing financial and estate planning landscape to ensure your family is protected and cared for when you cannot care for them yourself.

She has helped families protect their vulnerable loved ones, leave plans for their estates after their deaths, and grieve the deaths of their loved ones exclusively for nearly a decade.

Prior to law school, Sarah attended Oklahoma State University in Stillwater, Oklahoma and Putnam City High School in Oklahoma City, Oklahoma. She is truly "made in Oklahoma" and is uniquely qualified to understand the needs and challenges of Oklahoma families.

Sarah practices Brazilian Jiu Jitsu at Redline Academy in Edmond, Oklahoma with her limited free time.

She comes from a family with a public service background, and believes strongly in fighting for the rights of every family, of every income level, in Oklahoma.

The apples of her eye are her two young, energetic, sons and two mostly well-behaved dogs

Connect with Sarah C. Stewart and Solid Serenity Legal Solutions

I really appreciate you reading my book! Here are my social media coordinates:

Friend me on Facebook:
http://facebook.com/sarahstewartlaw
Subscribe to my blog:
http://www.solidserenity.com
Connect on LinkedIn:
http://www.linkedin.com/in/sarahstewartlaw
Visit my website:
http://www.solidserenity.com